Parental Suicide

What, When, How to Tell the Children

Carol Hoyt, R.N. and Susan Hart-Hester, Ph.D.

Parental Suicide: What, When, How to Tell the Children
© 2024 Carol Hoyt, R.N. and Susan Hart-Hester, Ph.D.

ISBN 979-8-35095-842-3
eBook ISBN 979-8-35095-843-0

Contents

Acknowledgements

A special thank you to grand-daughter Kennedy Laughy
for the original illustrations

Poetry by Susan Hart-Hester

If crying changed the end result

Then the buckets filled

Could spill their worth

For a better word of reason

Introduction

When a suicide of a loved one occurs, there is little comfort in those first dark gray hours of disbelief. In the clouds of reality that day, what and how to tell a child about mommy or daddy's death will seem like an insurmountable task. How can I tell them he killed himself? I want to be truthful, but I want to spare them too much heartache. How can I do this when I am barely functioning myself? I found myself in this situation in January of 1994 when my twenty-seven-year-old son chose suicide by way of carbon monoxide poisoning in the car in his garage. Our son, Eddie, left behind an eighteen-month-old boy, Garrett. This is how I became involved with what, when, and how to tell the children of a parent's suicide. There is information out there on childhood grief but very little with direct regard to suicide. We asked survivors to share their memories of going through this situation as a child. Information from letters and interviews has been of tremendous help to us in formulating this book.

This is a guide that you can identify with because it is written by someone who has gone through the same thing you are experiencing now. It speaks in words you can understand and with the empathy of knowing what you now face. I remember, in the blur of what was happening around me, Garrett, although only 18 months of age at the time, clinging to me. I can remember feeling very desperate that I needed an immediate way to handle this. I wanted some idea of what to do, and how to present this to Garrett in a way that was appropriate for his age. I needed a long range look at what could be planned for the future. I guess in an instant, I saw all the delayed grief, anger, and loss he may feel in the future. It terrified me because I was in the midst of it now, as you are. I was hurt, scared and devastated all at once. I wanted it all not to be true. I wanted to wake up from this excruciating nightmare to find out that it was JUST a nightmare. One of those dreams where you wake up shaking and sweating, where the lion had almost eaten you and you were exhausted from the chase. Denial creeping up my chest. Keeping it a secret, then sometimes exploding it out loud. "Not my Eddie, not when we couldn't see it. Not without a warning, a sign. He wouldn't do this, wouldn't leave his parents, his little boy, his brothers. How could he have been hurting and been this depressed that we hadn't seen it?" Regrettably, this scenario happens over 45,000 times a year to people just like you and me.

I needed someone to say, "Carol, there is help out there. Here is a book that will be a guideline for telling your little boy about his daddy." Hopefully, this book will provide some answers to other surviving parents, grandparents, caregivers and friends. Our sincere thanks and continued healing.

I press the memories of who you used to be

Between the pages of my heart

And then I start to cry

For I hear the thoughts you tried

So hard to hide.

Goodbye.

Dear Eddie,

You are still very near to my heart, as I sit here in the chilly October morning sunlight, watching Garrett gleefully playing out on the deck. It was only yesterday that you were here running with the same childlike abandonment… or was it a million years ago? He reminds me so very much of you, always inquisitive and exploring by nature, having to learn everything by doing. Has it really been only nine months since you decided life was too painful for you to bear any longer?

The joy of carrying you in my womb for nine months and the depth of grief felt these last nine have no correlation. Perhaps, only a lesson in the total eclipse of emotions felt by a human being. I never expected to feel this kind of grief through you, son. Now in raising Garrett in your place, I have the added responsibility of answering his soon to be asked questions of, "Why did daddy leave me?" I pray you will be very near in spirit to guide me in my responses. (Written by Carol Hoyt before beginning this book.)

It's all that I can do

When I think of you

To stop the sighing

To halt the crying

That spills away the heartaches

In a river of my pain

Chapter One provides the foundation for understanding the impact that suicide can have on family and friends.

Chapter Two discusses developmental milestones from prenatal through infancy.

Chapter Three guides the reader through cognitive stages present from the toddler years to preschool ages.

Chapter Four addresses the emerging of the child from the first grade to the fifth grade where recognition of the permanence of death begins to develop.

Chapter Five presents the developing child through the middle school years struggling with self-doubt and relying significantly on peer approval.

Chapter Six discusses the emerging adolescent as newly reflective, perhaps acting out his or her feelings with aggression or hiding behind a mask of passivity.

Chapter Seven addresses straight talk from parent to parent about living through the loss of a loved one while trying to care for the needs of a child left behind by the parent's suicide.

Chapter Eight: Resources offers a *non-inclusive* list including Internet sites and local sources for support, albeit it reading materials or counseling.

Chapter Nine: Provides references used to compile information within the text.

This book is written for those of you who have experienced a recent suicide in your family and are now faced with what to tell the child left behind. The chapters are divided into specific age categories; included in each are stories and excerpts from conversations with people who have lived through the suicidal death of a parent or are a surviving parent or caregiver. Their paraphrased stories are in italics so you will know when they begin and end. This information is intended to be used as suggested strategies for the surviving parent or caregiver; knowing that each child who has survived a parental suicide is uniquely different and the events surrounding the death will vary greatly. There are still basic fundamental questions and concerns that we have attempted to cover. Our hope is that you will gain the insight and courage you need now to guide your child through the aftermath of a suicide. Perhaps our experiences will make the healing process a little easier.

Remembering our last time together

Christmas, December 25th, 1993

Eddie came to our house on Christmas with gifts (he always brought gifts for everyone.) He was well dressed in khaki pants and a nicely ironed beige shirt. His face was full and cheeks were rosy. He looked healthy but somewhat different – a little stressed. Maybe I'm just trying to remember a sign of what he was thinking or planning.

He seemed to enjoy seeing Garrett, picking him up, holding him, and giving him toys he had bought him. My stomach hurts even now; 26+ years later when I think back on this "last time." Why couldn't I have seen what was going to happen in just 13 more days? Why couldn't he have said "Mom, I'm thinking about suicide, I need help, please, help me." Why couldn't he have hugged me and laid his head on my shoulder and told me how miserable he was? Where were his friends? Someone, anyone? Depression is the great isolator, the deceiver of emotion.

Eddie had planned to play golf with his friend the night before his suicide. But, according to the letter we found after his death, he voices how he had been thinking about suicide for a while. He even asked us to forgive him and asked us to love and care for his son Garrett.

This brought it all together for me on the "mask of depression." It was concealed so well, no one thought he would ever kill himself. No one dreamed he would end his life – but he did.

When darkness comes to steal your joy
Let the days lived bear witness
To lift his spirit through the memories
Locked inside your head

CHAPTER ONE:

Understanding Suicide

Although no official U.S. data are compiled on the effect suicide has on family, friends and relative survivors, it is estimated that each suicide influences a minimum of six to as many as 35 other people (Suicide.org). Based upon CDC data posted by the American Foundation for Suicide Prevention (afsp.org), 45,979 Americans died by suicide in 2020, with 1.2 million citizens having attempted suicide. However, *suicide is a global issue.* According to data (2019) from the World Health Organization, suicide accounted for 1.3% of all deaths worldwide making it the 17th leading cause of death (https://www.who.int/publications). According to National Institutes of Health research, an estimated 7,000 to 30,000 children lose a parent to suicide each year (in the United States). Although, the numbers may be actually higher due to the manner in which the death is recorded – accidental versus suicide. As shared through personal memories, presenting the death as accidental may only intensify grief and feelings of anger and/or betrayal down the road. Truly, silence will not heal the pain in your heart.

A woman who was sixteen when her father committed suicide described the aftermath.

This young woman talked about how astonishing it was that after her parent's suicide there was no one talking or explaining anything to her about it. This left her mind racing and wondering what really happened. It became a "nightmarish" type dream that intensified her grief. She describes how this loneliness had a silence to it like being deaf.

Who attempts suicide? As we learned with Eddie, there is no predictable face to suicide. While many suicidal parents demonstrate common behavior patterns that may be used for prevention, a number of behaviors are co-existing with other disorders making detection difficult. Although women attempt suicide more often than men, nearly four times more males successfully commit suicide. Firearms are the most common suicide method. In fact, among children below the age of eleven, a gun is the weapon most thought about when contemplating suicide. More teenagers are *attempting* suicide using drugs and/or over the counter medications they find readily available; therefore, it is extremely important to know the environment in which your child lives. Are there guns accessible? Are you monitoring access to medications, including over the counter drugs? *Are medications placed in a safe cabinet, out of reach from the child?* Think ahead to the ways that prevention can make your home and surroundings a safer haven for your child.

As we have researched the literature and talked to other survivors of suicide since Eddie's death, we know that everyone grieves differently. *This shocking and painful loss of your loved one must be grieved according to your timeline.* If you are reading this book, then you have an added layer to manage, for you are dealing with a child's grief alongside your own. As we have seen through our readings and interviews, the developmental level and age of a child are important factors in their understanding of a parental loss. *We needed to know how to talk to Garrett. We needed to know what to say and how to say it.* We know children feel the loss of a parent. They feel guilt, anger, blame, and a jumble of other emotions that cloud their interaction with you and others.

At times it will seem like an overwhelming task for you to try to think about the emotions of your child when your own feelings are so painful. Because you have sought out this book and are reading, it says a lot about where your thoughts are with concern for your child. You will be able to do this! I have to say that there were two of us, my husband and myself as Garrett's caregivers and later as his adoptive parents. You will do the right thing in handling the subject of suicide with your children. A lot of what happens will depend on how well your grief is resolved. It is very important for you to get help for yourself, too!

Nowhere could I lean, not one strong hand

Outreached to catch the shreds of my soul

Now scattered across the landscape of this empty form

CHAPTER TWO:

Prenatal Through Infancy

"I really don't know how to start. Yes, my father committed suicide, but I never even met him. I know that my mother and my two brothers were more affected by it because they knew him. But just because I didn't know him doesn't mean I'm not affected. Sometimes I feel sorry for myself. I look at pictures taken of his grave the day of the funeral. I think that it isn't fair that I never met him. I think maybe he would have loved me a lot. He never had a daughter before. Maybe he would have spoiled me and we would have done things together. Maybe I would have been 'Daddy's little girl.' But then that probably wouldn't have happened anyway because he was an alcoholic. My mother remarried a month before I turned five. My step-father is a wonderful person deep inside but he doesn't show his love very often. Sometimes I wonder what my life would have been like if my father were here.

I also have this guilty feeling about his death. I imagine that he didn't want another child or maybe he felt he couldn't handle it emotionally. These reasons could have led him to kill himself. I had a really hard time with these feelings when I hit junior high age. Seeing certain commercials of a father and daughter would cause me to break into tears. Just recently my father's mother died. She was old and we knew it was coming. When I started crying one day shortly thereafter and couldn't stop, my husband asked why. I felt like my grandmother was the last connection with my father. She would always show me pictures and such, but now that she was gone, I was afraid that whole part of my soul would go with her. It is kind of like that feeling I get when I go to the cemetery. Here I am sitting at the grave of a man I never met. I'm crying yet wondering, 'Who was this man? Did he smell good like aftershave or bad like alcohol? Did people like him? Did he speak his mind? Was he a good dad to my brothers? A good husband to my mother?' I'll never know these answers except from someone else's point of view. So, all I can do is look at the grave and cry and wonder. My mother is sort of quiet about the whole thing. This really hurt my brothers bad. They both battle alcoholism today and I think it stems from this. One breaks down when he thinks about it and the other won't even talk about it. I am 25 years old and have never even discussed this with my whole family – just my mother who I feel is an incredibly strong woman for having gone through all of this. She has done a wonderful job as my mom. I know without her I could really be messed up. I guess that sums it up. Suicide sure does affect people's lives. If the person doing it only realized what was going to happen afterwards, maybe they would feel loved enough to stick around. I know I would."

Even though this woman was not yet borne when her father committed suicide, her words express a feeling of loss and confusion. Although the terms "prenatal guilt" and "prenatal loss" seem inconceivable, this young mother of two clearly felt these emotions. Her mother was just five months pregnant when her father made his decision. As she wrote, "*just because I didn't know him doesn't mean I'm not affected."* This woman identifies early feelings of loss, guilt, and fear. Unlike many older surviving children, she (and others like her) has an image of her father built from another's point of view. She said her grandmother would tell her stories and show her pictures. Happy funny stories gave her a connection to the man she understood to be her father.

> *Here I am sitting at the grave of a man I never met.*
>
> *I'm crying and yet wondering, "Who was this man?"*
>
> *"Did he smell good like aftershave or bad like alcohol?"*

Reflections from this young woman are validated through her experiences with family. She continues to adjust to feelings of loss, anger and blame even today. What seems important to identify from her experience is the need to share truthful information about the death of a parent early on in a child's life. What emotional bond was formed with the surviving parent during infancy? This young mother was told of her father's death but did not have adequate support mechanisms as she progressed through the process of grieving toward acceptance. Expressions of denial by her older siblings fostered additional feelings of blame and guilt. Growing into young adulthood carrying mixed pictures of a father she never knew complicated her acceptance of his death. Watching family members develop behavior problems, i.e., gambling and alcohol use added to the blurred view of what happened to her dad. As survivors, we all cross this threshold of denial. We watch other loved ones move through the grief process. How can we help them? How can we help ourselves?

Providing care for a child who has lost a parent, while we too, are grieving is perhaps the hardest job imaginable. We continue to work towards a better understanding of the what, when and how to talk to children during this time of grief. Caregivers can share stories and memorabilia with surviving children that strengthen the connection to the parent. It seems important to build a vivid picture full of images that encompass all the senses. Can the fragrance of a favorite aftershave be a part of that image? Yes, it can.

These reflections nurture a positive connection between the parent and child. Looking at pictures and listening to stories gives the child a foundation for knowing his or her parent. They will explore the history of a parent who laughed, cried, and played just like they do. We all need this sense of connection. Clearly, infants build upon this connection from birth.

The term "infant" comes from a Latin term meaning incapable of speech. Literally, infants learn through their senses – hearing, tasting, touching, smelling and feeling. During the grieving process, children can absorb the emotional feelings of the surviving parent or caregiver.

While an infant does not understand the concept of death, they still react to the fear of separation. A baby builds a connection with a certain way of being held, your smell, your voice, and even within a few weeks, your face. Babies react to your emotions. They respond to your "baby talk" – cooing readily at the sound of your voice. A baby also reacts to other emotions such as crying. They can feel the tenseness of your body as you deal with the loss of a loved one. They may even develop physical signs, such as skin rashes, vomiting and diarrhea.

Eight days after Eddie's death, Garrett started vomiting. This sickness persisted for two days. He would not let anyone hold him except my husband Edd or myself. I sat in a rocking chair near exhaustion, while relatives stood by helplessly. A baby will not understand your grief, *only react to it.* Projections of intense emotion and feelings may have a lasting effect on the development of the infant's perception of self. Therefore, be aware of how your emotions are expressed around your child.

Initially, babies experience "pleasure learning," i.e., they find their thumb by accident and discover thumb sucking to be a pleasurable experience. Trial and error learning soon replaces random actions. At around twelve months, the baby's behavior becomes goal-oriented. He experiments with actions and reactions to achieve a desired effect. This ability signals the beginning of basic thinking skills. It is also during this developmental period that the infant becomes fearful of strangers, of being apart from the parent for any length of time. It seems vital to nurture another relationship with a close significant other (surviving parent, grandparent) during this time.

Routine is important for the child, especially during the first months following the death of a parent. The chaos created during the initial discovery, the funeral plans, and police reports, all takes its toll on everyone. Exposure to the sense of grief and loss is inevitable; therefore. maintaining routines of naps and playtime provides the baby with a greater sense of security. Although the familiar voice is gone, the pattern of feeding, nap, and play is the same. The rocking chair still rocks as she falls off to sleep and the music box plays the same soft lullaby. A baby whose parent is gone needs the security blanket offered through familiar voices and surroundings.

Advice for helping your baby adjust:

WHAT:

- A picture of the deceased parent in a prominent place & referring to it as the child's mommy/daddy;
- Identifying characteristics of the child that are like his parent, i.e., eye/hair color, smile or laugh.

WHEN:

- As soon as possible. This will help you get used to seeing pictures of the deceased around too; if this is too painful for you, keep a scrapbook or box of mementos that the child can look through later.

HOW:

- A baby will not comprehend the concept of death as final and irreversible
- Connect the baby with familiar voices, surroundings and significant others
- Routine is very important now. Continue to maintain familiar patterns (sleeping, eating, bathing, etc.) as best you can.

Such loss fed a canyon of death

Weakening my resolve

To understand when

I would breathe again

CHAPTER THREE:

Preschoolers (2–5 years)

A mother we spoke with describes to her child that their dad had a "sickness" that caused him great pain in his head. It wasn't like being sick with a cold or sore throat. He had gone to the doctor about it many times, and finally, because the doctors couldn't make him well, he gave up hope and ended his pain.

Experiences with death are very limited for young children. Developmentally, children build new knowledge based upon what they have learned at a previous level. They respond to a situation based upon what they do know. If a toddler is told that "daddy died," he may think only that Daddy is sleeping. The concept of death has no permanence. Daddy has disappeared. Death must be associated with separation. A toddler will not comprehend the irreversibility of death. Say directly, "daddy has died" but know that you will have to repeat yourself again and again.

Conversations with a small child should be in concrete terms which relate to their current level of development. Avoid saying things like, "daddy got really sick and died" or "mommy is sleeping, passed on, or was taken from us." These terms can be very confusing to a small child since they think only in direct terms. Telling a child that daddy was taken from you connotes images of monsters or bad guys. Youngsters may think, "if bad guys can take somebody as big and strong as daddy then they would carry me away too!" Also, if "mommy is sleeping," then they think she must wake up at some point. The child may begin to be afraid of going to sleep because their parent went to sleep and hasn't awakened and they fear that may happen to them too. If you tell the child that daddy got sick, they might think that they will die if they get sick, or that you will die if you say you are sick.

Even at this early stage, we personally recommend using the word "dead." We started telling Garret that his daddy had died and as devout Christians we would include "daddy in heaven" during his nightly prayers. Garrett continued to talk about his first daddy from the very start. I know this is so very hard to do since so many emotions are flowing. Time and time again when the words would not come for me, I would just hold Garrett and rock, letting him know how much I would be here for him.

For Garrett, his dad exists as an angel who watches over him. Although the concepts of angels and heaven are abstract, Garrett builds images from our own reflections shared with him. One Sunday in church Garrett leaned against me and said "daddy is sitting next to me." I asked him how he knew this and he said, "Because he is an angel and angels can do anything." Others may state that talk of heaven is too abstract for a preschooler and that it leads to magical thinking, i.e., daddy will return. We believed in establishing a strong spiritual foundation for Garrett. Believing in a higher being will provide the building blocks of belief in himself.

As with the babies, toddlers need reassurance brought by routine. Explain to them why so many people are in the house (before and after the funeral.) We told Garrett that "lots of people love us and want to show us." Although family and friends tried hard to provide extra attention, Garrett needed us at this point. We drew as much of a safety net around him as we could.

For toddlers, the world is represented through symbolic thinking, i.e., they can represent objects, events or situations with mental pictures, words or gestures. However, preschoolers still have limited cognitive development. One limitation occurs in self-centered thinking and behaviors. Their world still revolves around their needs and wants; however, their ability to express those needs has improved. The ability to develop a mental image enables them to derive feelings internally instead of reacting solely to external forces. Children at this stage rely on previous experiences as well as imagination to deal with feelings of loss or separation. Still, death has little permanence. These youngsters may use the word death but seem quite indifferent to its true meaning. Children at this age may see characters on television who "die" and then come back to life; therefore, death is reversible.

By the time your child is five years old, death has greater meaning. He may ask more questions about death, wanting to know how mommy died. Garrett related his dad's death to things he had seen on television, like a car wreck or a gun shot. He tested his reality a little more, venturing into a world where his imagination offered solutions and different ways to cope with new feelings of sorrow.

At five years old Garrett had no trouble expressing whenever the feeling hits him that "I really miss daddy, Eddie." We have looked at a familiar picture of Garrett on my lap with his dad sitting beside us and talked about his feeling of sadness. I have stated that I too, am sad about his death and I miss him as well. I also say things like, "wasn't your dad good looking? He had blond hair and his eyes were blue. He liked to play baseball and football a lot and was very good at both games." We also reminisce about when Eddie was a baby and where we lived and what room was his... Garrett seems to like hearing about his father. He asked us about how he died and we have told him that Eddie died because he breathed the smoke that comes out of the back of a car engine. His response was incredible, "but why didn't he hold his breath?" at five years old I still couldn't bring myself to say the word suicide, so I said "I don't know why. He was just so very sad." Know that sometimes you won't know the "right" words to say but at least be open and communicate with your child.

Another mother we spoke with explained to her children that even though dad is not here anymore, he is always with them spiritually. She told them about his "sickness" which caused him terrible pain and caused him to not think right. He so wanted the pain to stop but couldn't get it to subside. He ended his life to cease the pain. She tells her children that this is never the way, that there are ways to get help. She believed in telling her kids the truth about why their dad isn't with them anymore. She believed not lying to them was better for them.

This same mother realized that it was either going to be all out in the open, gently but honestly, or she would be tripping over what was said for years to come. She taught us that *"kids handle truth better than most would imagine. Truth is empowering."* I cried over her shared experiences. The insightfulness of this woman was incredible. Here in her own grief journey, she has such an open and honest relationship with her children. How inspiring I found her to be with my thoughts of telling Garrett about the death of his dad. Finally, I was reminded that suicide was indeed a clinical illness, not some mystery phenomenon that happens to a person. Her husband and father to her children, was ill at no fault of his own. So, it wasn't fair to blame him.

Advice for helping your toddler adjust:

WHAT:

- Symbolic thinking e.g., Daddy is only sleeping
- Death is not permanent e.g., mommy will come back
- Self-centered thinking: the world revolves around their wants and needs

WHEN: As soon as possible

HOW:

- Use direct terms; Daddy has died – be prepared to repeat this many times.
- Do not say dad or mom got sick, is lost, is sleeping or was taken from us.
- Keep pictures around for the child to remember his/her parent or keep a scrapbook
- Routine is still very important as it brings reassurance
- If death is a mystery to a child and his questions are ignored – fear increases due to the unknown.
- Encourage talking about the deceased parent. Share happy stories.

The heavens opened with a kiss

And offered a new home

A place that filled the empty space

You carried for so long

No sorrow now, no tears renew

For his hands reached down

And saved me too

CHAPTER FOUR:

Elementary (6-11 years)

We spoke with a woman who was just six years old when her mother committed suicide. She confirms in her experience that no one explained anything to her sibling or herself. They were taken away to other family caretakers and kept until after the funeral. They were then told that their mother had only passed away. I can only imagine the questions these kids had about what happened. Today this woman fantasizes about her life being different – had her mom lived. Why are so many people silent about telling the kids? To them, is it easier to deal with, or what?

At this age three important factors influence social development: the home, the school, and the child's peer group. Each factor plays a vital role in shaping the child's behavior, personality, and development. The child will start to ask much more concrete questions, e.g., "How did he die?" "Was he shot?" "Where was I when daddy died?"

We began showing Garrett videos of his "first Daddy," as we are calling Eddie. Garrett's reaction was very calm when we spoke about the way his dad looked. We asked him questions; how he felt about being able to see videos of his daddy when he was alive. We made sure he understood these videos were from the past. Children at this age can be confused about what is real on television or videos. Stressing the difference is very important. You do not want your child thinking that this person they see on the screen will return next week. In the process of watching these videos together, I held Garrett beside me on the couch. It could be a good idea to watch the videos first by yourself if you have not seen them since the death of your loved one. For me, having Garrett close was a comfort in viewing for the first time since Eddie's death. I always feel stronger when I have to be for him. I suppose it is the mothering instinct in me. Slowly, as Garrett wishes to see more, we will show him all the videos we have of Eddie. Living in this age and having access to technology as we do, Garrett can view videos of his father as a baby, watch Eddie play baseball and football. He can watch Eddie holding him as a newborn and see how loving Eddie was to him as the camera caught them playing together. As we watched the video with Garrett, I thought how lucky we were to have these vivid memories to share.

At six years old, Garrett attended kindergarten. We did not hear any peer related talk regarding his first daddy's death and the aspect of suicide. In future years, soon maybe, some child at school will make a remark or perhaps tease Garrett in some way about it. I hope by that time we will have prepared him to understand the truth and accept the often-harsh realities that go with it. The information we have received indicates that people are indeed desperate for ways to tell the children left behind.

I understand this feeling, for it has been mine – I OWN this feeling. But, with good intentions, we plunge onward, trying to consciously think before responding and planning our replies to Garrett's questions to the best of our abilities. Always with Garrett's feelings in mind first and foremost. We want to make this as easy as we can for him. No child should have to bear the anguish of a parental suicide alone with no one to help wipe away their tears and answer their questions- yet so many do.

A child in this developmental stage may feel responsible for the parent's death because they thought or said something hurtful to the parent. Make sure this child does not feel responsible in any way for the parent's suicide. Our way of answering this with Garrett has been – *"This was a sickness that caused your daddy to become so sad and unhappy that he thought to kill himself would be the answer. It's a different kind of sadness, you or I have never been this sad. It makes you where you can't think of anything happy. Your mind doesn't think right. Your Daddy could only think of stopping his sadness—by killing himself. It is a sickness of the mind. And it made him make a very bad choice. This is never ever a good way to solve your problems."*

Youngsters at this stage of development are particularly vulnerable to the loss of a parent to suicide. Their cognitive skills enable them to recognize the irreversibility of death, yet they seem unable to deal with the possibilities of that parent's return, of monsters, of bad guys, of getting sick and dying too.

We are aware of what happens at Garrett's school by staying in close contact with Garrett's teachers. This is of course important for you to do with any child, but in the case of a parental suicide, it is even more vital. We let the teacher know what had happened to Eddie. We established a positive link between the school and our home. This enables us to handle any problems with behavior, academics, or peer interactions that might surface at a later date. The school counselor is also an important variable in the child's adjustment process. Often, for children this young, it is not what they say, but what they *do* that tells you the most about their feelings. Some children may regress to "baby" like behavior, requiring more attention. Other children might become aggressive and act out their frustrations by getting into fights or refusing to comply with teacher requests. You should also talk daily to your child about what happened in school, on the bus, in the lunchroom, on the playground. We can find out a lot of information from our children by this simple routine.

At this age, some youngsters may *seem* to deny that a death has actually occurred, or at least they may *appear* to place little significance to it. Just because children appear to be conducting life as usual, they are, in their own ways, grieving. Don't forget to recognize their grief, although disguised.

> *Having no information on a mother's suicide and finding out about it from other people was another way a child went through this experience. Denying it ever happened and making up another excuse for her parent's death was one way a woman we interviewed handled her situation. While the surviving parent was dealing with their grief, she was sent to live with people she didn't even know. The grief this child felt could have caused the pneumonia and hospitalization that occurred shortly after her mom's death. She was absolutely in the dark about all matters concerning her mom's death.*

Include the children in the funeral plans and preparations as much as possible. Explain what will happen at the service, perhaps that many people will be crying, preparing them for all the emotions that culminate at this time. What will happen to Mommy's or Daddy's body? What is a casket? They might have a special way they would like to remember their deceased parent either during the funeral or at a later date or more private time for them. Ask your child, but know you may have to help them at this age with an idea of something that they can do. By including the child at the funeral which is our "mourning ritual or saying goodbye ritual", we can allow our child to recognize the realness of the death and feel supported by people who love them. This can be the beginning of healing together.

Suggestions for helping your child:

WHAT:

- Child sees death as a taker or spirit that comes and gets you
- Fear that death is contagious and other loved ones will catch it and die too
- Fascinated with issues of mutilation; very curious about what the body looks like
- Connects death with violence and may ask, "Who killed him?"
- Think there are 3 categories of people who die: elderly, handicapped, klutzes
- Asks concrete questions
- Feels guilt – may blame self for parent's death
- May worry how the deceased can eat or breathe, etc.
- Continues to have difficulty expressing feelings verbally
- May show increased aggression
- Defends against feeling helpless
- Somatic symptoms
- School phobia (especially if single parent)
- Continues to have difficulty comprehending abstractions such as heaven, spirituality

WHEN: As soon as possible

HOW:

- Talk openly with your child, if you don't have an answer, say so.
- Ask questions.
- Make sure child does not feel responsible for parent's death.
- Identify child's specific fears, e.g. "Are you afraid you will die too?"
- Provide opportunities for play, drawing, and art as means of expressing feelings. Are they acting out death scenes in play, playing violently, aggressively?

- Normalize feelings and fears, "It's ok to feel sad about daddy's death"
- Address distortions and perceptions; Help child share bad dreams
- Help child cope with impulse control
- Share positive memories of the deceased parent
- Model healthy coping behaviors
- Avoid clichés "don't worry, things will be ok", "You're such a strong boy"
- Use specific, concrete words, not euphemisms, avoid "daddy went to sleep"
- If a child is given the responsibility for the loss or the state of health of the surviving parent, fear increases
- When the same sex parent dies, fear of death increases even more
- It is ok for you to ask me any questions about Mommy or Daddy's death
- It is not your fault Mommy or Daddy committed suicide. Do you ever feel it is?
- Are you worried what will happen to us now that Daddy or Mommy is gone?
- It is okay to cry

Let the winds blow all the painful past
The moments that we pray won't last
Let all the seconds left be taken fast
By His saving second chances

CHAPTER FIVE:

Middle School (12–14 Years)

A mother wrote to us that people would say things to her 13-year-old such as, "things could be worse." You can only think, did they really think that saying this would help him? Most people are at a loss for words when comforting a grieving person from a relative's suicide. When Eddie died, our priest told me I wasn't the only one to go through something like that. This infuriated me to think that I wasn't the only one. Maybe I wanted to be the only one. My heart was cracking in two and the constant crying was exhausting me. Please just hold me and tell me it gets easier with time.

Adolescence is a rocky time for most youngsters as they experience rapid growth in height, weight, and physical characteristics. Best understood in three stages, adolescence covers a time span of approximately ten years: age 11 – 20+ years. For the pre-adolescent child, the onset of physical changes enhances self-consciousness. Many youngsters within the pre-adolescent age group (ages 11-13) experience an increased level of "clumsiness." Not all youngsters experience such heightened self-awareness to their physical changes; however, physical growth during adolescence is a developmental fact. What affect do all these physical changes have on the young child whose parent commits suicide?

While the pre-adolescent youngster appears to grow in physical stature, he is still a child mentally. Cognitively, the child sees things in a very concrete state. Abstract thinking is just starting to develop. Few youngsters can conceptualize beyond the here and now to attach meaning to present actions and future consequences.

Although the pre-adolescent child does differentiate the concept of living and non-living, death has an almost evil connotation. A youngster may deal with the suicidal death of his parent by blaming "bad guys" who entered the house and killed him. As the youngster enters mid-adolescence, he maintains his preoccupation with his physical changes and peer attitudes. Social acceptance from peers is an important element in the mid-adolescent's life.

One young girl, age ten at the time, talks about her feelings with her peers – She was in the 5th grade when she lost a parent to suicide. Her friends apparently were afraid of her because of the suicide. How horrible for this girl at an age where her world has suddenly changed now, she faces peer group bullying. She recommends only the "right time", not the "right age" to tell the child about a parent's suicide.

Self-centered thinking can lead the child to believe that his parent committed suicide because of something HE said or did. Often, the child will blame themselves for the death of their parent. Maybe he yelled at his dad, or didn't excel at football the way his dad did in school. All kinds of self-blaming thoughts may enter the cognitive picture, for the mid-adolescent child is caught between concrete thinking and the ability to test additional hypotheses regarding the death of his parent. When normal children are very angry, they often have death wishes. Magical thinking combined with guilt may bring the thought that they wished their loved one to death. If parents are unable to discuss the loss, the lack of parental communication may reaffirm the child's distorted beliefs.

One woman felt if someone would have just talked to her about her father's death by suicide, her life would have been so much easier.

Additionally, the youngster may not want to discuss the concepts of death and dying since these are personal issues that hit too close to home. What will his peers think of him if they know his father committed suicide? Will they think he is crazy? Will they think he will do the same? This child places greater emphasis on peer reactions than on parents and family members. In fact, suicide contagion following the suicide of a peer is more common for adolescents since they are more influenced by peer pressures and behaviors.

Youngsters left behind by the death of a parent may truly want to know "why" daddy killed himself. Their perception may be that the parent "had it all" i.e., home, family, job, so why would he kill himself? The adolescent might rationalize that his dad "had it all" and chose suicide to escape the pain, then maybe he could escape too.

Although the mid-adolescent child is developing the ability to reach moral judgments regarding right and wrong, he is often so caught up in his own self-centered reality that what is right happens to be whatever HE chooses to think is right.

Suggestions for helping your child adjust:

WHAT:

- Still a child mentally although rapid growth physically
- Sees everything concretely
- Death may have evil meaning
- Peer group and social acceptance is very important
- Self-blame for parent's death
- Concepts of death and dying are personal issues, the child may have difficulty discussing them.
- Values peer reactions greater than family members
- Suicide contagion is more common at this age

WHEN: As soon as possible

HOW

- Discuss death to sort out the child's distortions
- Talk about the child's feeling and your own
- Watch out for changes in his/her behavior
- Keep pictures available for the child to see and discuss
- No new changes at this time for the child e.g. moving
- Respect your child's confidences. Parents need to ask permission before talking to friends and relatives about their expressed grief.
- Have them participate in decisions relating to the deceased parent.
- Remember that children will have inconsistent responses and emotions.
- Be honest about your own limitation in understanding grief at this point.

My heart is full of winter's chill

As this land in barren stillness

Lies in silent mourning

For the warmth of a new dawn

CHAPTER SIX:

High School (15-18 Years)

For the young child entering late-adolescence, the concept of God and spirituality take on a new meaning. The ability to think abstractly adds to the power of a higher source over-riding the actions of the present. The deceased parent may be pictured as a guardian angel looking out for her.

A teenager we spoke with described her sorrow concerning her mom never being able to see the great events in a normal life. The graduation, marriage, and the future babies she will not get to meet. To ease her feelings on these losses, she pictures her mom as her guardian angel.

There may also be confusion over the ability of God to stop a parent from completing the suicide. Why couldn't such a powerful being stop his dad from pulling the trigger? There may be mixed feelings of regret and anger. The newly reflective teenager may seem rather passive with his anger or he may act out aggressively by getting involved in fights at school or around the home.

As the youngster reaches late-adolescence (17-20+) he has the cognitive ability to test alternate ideas and hypotheses regarding life's situations.

A 16-year-old girl we spoke with says it all depends on the other living parent in how the child develops their grief. If they see crying and losing it, they too, will react this way. But she thinks when they are older, they will again resist their grief. A 19-year-old tells us he felt the support from family and friends. Through this he realized that he alone knew how to get through this loss. He expressed how he would question the "what if's".

This young man has reached a state of "equilibrium," developing the ability to assess multiple possibilities within a given situation. He realizes that death will occur. He also realizes, although he may choose not to accept it, that the suicide death of his parent is not his fault. For although he has developed more complex cognitive abilities, he may choose to remain in a very concrete, self-centered realm. However, for the majority of youngsters entering this stage, the narcissism dominating the pre and mid adolescent years will dissipate. The child within this late stage develops a more reflective personality as he moves towards a more "other-centered" attitude. This increased ability to think abstractly makes the adolescent more vulnerable to life's pitfalls. The youngster becomes intensely interested in death, although they are afraid of the reality and finality of death. Youngsters tend to select music with lyrics about death and or attend movies built around the theme of death. The adolescent wants to know the truth about his parent's death. Such fascination with death exists concomitantly with a death of their own mortality. If my parent can die, then I can die too. This vulnerable stage of newly developed cognitive independence may be paired with the lingering doubt of self-worth and self-blame.

As a 17-year-old girl, this survivor told us she felt she was responsible for her father's death. Without going into details on why she felt responsible, she felt she would always feel this way. The way her living parent handled the suicide was pretty astonishing in that, in one days' time, their house was sold and they moved into a new one the very day after the funeral. Feeling she couldn't cry and she just had to stay strong. Her forever grieving his death with guilt was very moving to hear. I hope she receives the help she desperately needs.

Another 17-year-old indicated that "blame was the biggest problem" First, blaming himself, then blaming his surviving parent for not staying in the marriage.

As we mentioned, at all levels, it is important for you to help your child understand that he is not to blame for his parent's death. Nothing he said or did caused his dad to commit suicide. He can acknowledge that he exchanged heated words with his dad, or even wished his dad would die, but he must recognize that his words didn't cause his father's death. You may find yourself repeating this to your child again and again.

A 20-year-old woman shared that she has questions all the time about why her mom took her own life. How did she not love her enough to want to see her grow up? Maybe it was because she didn't love her mother enough? So many questions and never any answers. She relates that possibly there was another way for her mother to handle this. She obviously wanted to know the truth and details why.

Some teens around this age may cover up their feelings out of worry for the surviving parent. Outwardly, he seems fine. Inwardly, he feels alone and confused. Conversely, the adolescent may run away, become aggressive, promiscuous, take drugs, etc. all of these behaviors can be attempts to mask his feelings of sadness and confusion regarding the death of his parent.

Now as an adult woman looking back, this survivor says that perhaps telling the child the truth would make the grieving more natural. In her case, she had difficulty believing her parent was really gone. Now, as an adult, she grieves for him.

Suggestions for helping your child adjust:

WHAT

- Spirituality takes on new meaning.
- Confusion over God not preventing the suicide.
- Mixed feelings – passive or acting out.
- Tests alternate ideas and theories regarding life situations.
- Comes to a better realization that suicide of parent is not their fault, although blame may still be present.
- Self-centeredness starts to leave, moves toward other-centered attitude.
- Interested in death.
- Afraid of reality and finality of death.
- Wants to know truth with all details.
- May have lingering doubts of self-worth and self-blame.
- May cover up their feeling because of worry of other surviving parent

WHEN: As soon as possible

HOW

- Talk to your child about death and his/her feelings.
- Do not be afraid to express your own feelings of sadness, confusion, even blame, although do not make the child shoulder your grief, too.
- Keep pictures and momentos available
- Answer the child's questions about his/her parent's suicide truthfully.

CHAPTER SEVEN:

Parent to Parent Talk

Let's be honest here – this is an unbelievable situation you are in, you ache, you're angry, you can't stop crying and blaming yourself. You are hardly able to function. Then, you see your child. It is up to you now and you feel this enormous sense of "how am I going to do this?"

I'll tell you how I got through it.

First and foremost, I have a deep faith, more faith than I had known about or would outwardly admit to having before this tragedy. Believing that my loved one was now at peace and in God's arms helped me, after time, quiet the crying, aching, and seemingly real "hole in my heart."

Secondly, the love and support of family and friends became the medicine I needed for this devastating void I felt in my life at that time. I, who was always the strong one, now had to let others minister to me. I didn't resist, don't you either!

Thirdly, Garrett became my focus since he was the child left behind. In my grief – wanting to lighten his grief helped me work through my feelings. Our research (for Garrett and others like him) came to be a way to vent and, perhaps do something to help others. Others just like me who were plunged, unwillingly, into this situation of unparalleled sadness over the loss combined with the worry of what, when, and how to tell the children.

Counseling, if available, was another Godsend especially in my case since the counselor had also lost a child to suicide. Relating to someone who had been through this kind of loss is so important because I think it is different from other death loss grieving. You know they are speaking your language – know what your heart is telling your mind. I came to grips with a lot of factors during those agonizing hours of crying, talking, listening and sharing with this caring woman. One was the mysterious face of depression and how deceiving it can be. Realizing that indeed, acute depression/depletion of brain chemicals/low serotonin/whatever the term, had taken my son from me. The bright, athletic, handsome, outgoing, fun-loving, popular son of mine, had been depressed. Severely depressed, and I had missed it. And then the real clincher, it wasn't my fault! I thought it should be my fault since I was the one who talked to him the most, the one he came to with his problems – or so I thought.

Finally, time has helped. It is now been over twenty plus years since losing Eddie to suicide. There is still never a day that in some way I don't think of him but the painful feeling is not as apparent. I can laugh when I talk about him or memories pop up into my mind or I stumble upon something that was his. I can talk openly without tears welling up in my eyes with the mention of his name. No longer do I wake up with the dread of thinking about his death and being consumed by it. Time has been a healer and it will be for you, too. Allow yourself to grieve. Understand your own feelings and learn from others who have walked this path before you. Learn both the good and the bad. Promise yourself, every day, you will get through this and be true to yourself. You will find that you heal a little more with each passing day.

You might think that in reading how other people lived through a parental suicide when they were children does not apply in this day and age. You may believe that we are much more advanced in the way we deal with depression and suicide than we were twenty or thirty years ago. Yes, we have come a long way in most people's perception of what depression is and why suicide occurs. But we must continue to inform other people about depression and that it must be treated, and that there is no shame in seeking treatment.

Unless you have experienced the suicidal death of a close loved one, you do not fully comprehend the enormous impact it has on someone's life, forever. Dealing with it in a healthy forum is vitally important. We can never again return to the past, when it was taboo to talk about and closeted forever, leaving survivors with decades of unresolved grief and pain. There is a legacy to suicide and there is no way around that part, but it should no longer be that "conspiracy of silence." Instead, we can give our children an "understanding with openness."

It has taken me a long time to come to grips with Eddie's suicide. There is so much pain and grief involved. I read and hear about so many people committing suicide even today. With all the social media and instant messaging there is today it almost seems like I am seeing weekly notifications about people posting about their deceased loved ones they lost to suicide. My heart aches for each one of them because I feel what they are going through. Not to the degree that it impacted me over twenty plus years ago, but seeing posts like these do bring back those horrifying feelings. I think about the family it touches and how they are managing. I have flash backs of friends coming over, and worrying about Garrett who was just 18 months old at the time. I remember hugging my husband Edd and seeing his heart breaking into pieces. I see our two other sons showing their strength and faith at this time. Now I am seeing the long-term effects of this in one of them. How this act of depression is still there years later for some and not so much for others. Is it one person's coping skills over another or what? I think for me, my best coping method was knowing I had to take care of a child who needed me more now than ever. This could explain my love for him, to this day and why I've "over-parented" him maybe. I didn't think I was doing this at the time but I did. I'm not apologizing for it or consider it wrong. It's just that I have always felt I was given this child to raise and I better do my utmost best to give love, guidance, support and discipline. Sometimes it has been very challenging but always a joy. And most of all a reminder of Eddie. Maybe I over did it; they don't call me "helicopter mom" for nothing.

Garrett is now grown with a family of his own. I believe he now has a healthy outlook on what happened so many years ago. He is able to talk about his biological father's suicide with an adult attitude on depression and life choices. He is not a person who will let this negatively influence his life. Garrett says, "I'm not a person who gets soft-hearted about a personal tragedy." To me, this may be a defense mechanism he has put up, but it seems like a good one for him. He's dealt with a lot during his lifetime so far. To say he's been totally unscathed would be incorrect. We all just try to do the best we can in life and support each other.

Just be open with your children on a parental suicide and remember, you are not alone!

Heaven heals the broken wing

And seals an empty heart

With joyful songs to sing

CHAPTER EIGHT:

Resources

We have attempted to include some resources that provide information and/or support related to suicide, suicide prevention, and/or coping after loss due to suicide. *The list is not exhaustive and is not meant to indicate an endorsement of materials provided or sold via any of the listings.*

1. Suicide Support Groups: Best found through your local Mental Health Association or through local churches. Some groups may have a listing in the phone book or a website on the Internet. The American Association of Suicidology maintains a directory of support groups by state.

2. Compassionate Friends
   www.compassionatefriends.org

3. Suicide Associations and Alliances:

   a. American Association of Suicidology
      https://suicidology.org/
      1-800-275-TALK

   b. American Foundation for Suicide Prevention
      https://afsp.org/

    c. International Association for Suicide Prevention
https://www.iasp.info/

    d. Association for Death Education and Counseling
https://www.adec.org

    e. National Alliance for Grieving Children
www.childrengrieve.org

4. Center for Suicide Prevention—988 Suicide and Crisis Lifeline
https://988lifeline.org

5. Local Mental Health Organizations: Look under state/local government in phone book, find by category in yellow pages or search via Internet under local or state agencies

6. Local Churches/Pastors – check your area for listings – some churches sponsor grief counseling and/or grief support groups

7. School counselors – your local school district may provide resources for coping and understanding the grieving process

8. Local Police Departments Ask for Victims Assistance unit

9. Journals:

    a. *Suicide and Life-Threatening Behavior*
(https://onlinelibrary.wiley.com/journal/1943278x)

    b. *Archives of Suicide Research*
(https://www.tandfonline.com/loi/usui20)

10. Additional Websites

    a. Suicide Awareness Voices of Education (SAVE)
(https://save.org/)

    b. National Institute of Health: www. nih.org

    c. Child Mind Institute (https://childmind.org/)

    d. After Talk (www.aftertalk.com)

  e. Suicide Prevention Lifeline.org

  f. Our House (grief support centers) https://www.our-house-grief.org/

  g. Bereaved Parents of the USA (www.bereavedparentsusa.org)

11. The Dougy Center: National Center for Grieving Children and Families

   https://www.dougy.org

CHAPTER NINE:

References

These references are not intended as an exhaustive list but are offered as supportive documentation for content shared within this book. Our advice/recommendations are based upon our experiences and we want to remind the reader that each situation carries its own circumstances and responses/actions may need to vary based upon these variables.

Adam, K., Bouckomos, A., & Streiner, D. (1982). Parental loss and family stability in attempted suicide. *Arch Gen Psychiatry,* 39(9): 1081-1085.

American Academy of Child and Adolescent Psychiatry. Suicide in Children and Teens. https://www.aacap.org/AACAP/Families_and_Youth/Facts_for_Families/FFF-Guide/Teen-Suicide-010.aspx

Anju, M and Subha, N. (2013) Psychosocial stressors and patterns of coping in adolescent suicide attempts. Indian J Psychol Med. Jan-Mar; 35(1): 39-46.

Ann and Robert Lurie Children's Hospital of Chicago. Supporting grieving children. https://www.luriechildrens.org/en/patients-visitors/resources-support-services-for-families/bereavement-support/supporting-grieving-children/. Accessed: January 2020

Baker, J. & Sedney, M. (1996). How bereaved children cope with loss: An overview. In Corr, C. and Corr, D. (Ed.), Handbook of childhood death and bereavement, pp. 109-130. New York: Springer.

Beautrais, A., Joyce, P., & Mulder, R. (1996). Risk factors for serious suicide attempts among youths aged 13 through 24 years. *J Am Acad Child Adolesc Psychiatry*, 35(9): 1174-82.

Boergers, J., Spirito, A., & Donaldson, D. (1998). Reasons for adolescent suicide attempts: Associations with psychological functioning. *J Am Acad Child Adolesc Psychiatry*, 37(12): 1287-93.

Bolton, I., with Mitchell, C. (1984). My son, my son: A guide to healing after suicide in the family. Atlanta, GA: Bolton Press.

Bower, T. (1977). A primer on infant development. San Francisco, CA: W.H. Freeman

Bridge JA, Asti L, Horowitz LM, et al. (2015). Suicide Trends Among Elementary School-Aged Children in the United States From 1993 to 2012. *JAMA Pediatr*; 169:673.

Cain A. & Fast, I. (1966). Children's disturbed reactions to parent suicide. *American Journal of Orthopsychiatry*, 36, 873-880.

Cain, A. & Fast, I. (1972). Survivors of suicide. Springfield, IL: Charles C. Thomas.

Centers for Disease Control. Suicide among children, adolescents, and young adults United States, 1980-1992. *Monthly Morbidity and Mortality Weekly Report*, 44:289-91.

Center to Prevent Handgun Violence. (1998). Firearm Facts. Washington, D.C.

Cerel, J., Brown, M., Maple, M., Singleton, M., van de Venne, J., Moore, M., Flagerty, C. (2018). How many people are exposed to suicide? Not six. https://onlinelibrary.wiley.com/doi/full/10.1111/sltb.12450

Corr, C. and Corr, D. (1996). Handbook of Childhood Death and Bereavement. New York: Springer Publishing.

Cotton, C. and Range, L. (1990). Children's death concepts: Relationship to cognitive functioning, age, experience with death, fear of death, and hopelessness. J of Clinical Child Psychology, 19:123-127.

Cotton, C. and Range, L. (1993). Suicidality, hopelessness, and attitudes toward life and death in children. *Death Studies*, 17:185-191.

Dunne, E., McIntosh, J., Dunne-Maxim, K. (1987). Suicide and its Aftermath: Understanding and counseling the survivors. New York: Norton.

Fact Sheet. American Association of Suicidology. (2017). Washington, D.C. Accessed: January 2020

Feldman, M. & Wilson, A. (1997). Adolescent suicidality in urban minorities and its relationship to conduct disorders, depression, and separation anxiety. *Journal of the American Academy of Child and Adolescent Psychiatry*, 36(1): 75-84.

Glow, K. (2015). How to talk to your kids about death. https://www.goodhousekeeping.com/life/parenting/a32914/how-to-talk-to-kids-about-death/

Gordon, S. (2019). Kids often use OTC in suicide attempts. https://www.webmd.com/mental-health/addiction/news/2019

Gould, M., Fisher, P., Parides, M., Flory, M., & Shaffer, D. (1996). Psychosocial risk factors of child and adolescent completed suicide. *Arch General Psychiatry*, 53:1155-1162.

Graham, J. (2013). How do children comprehend the concept of death? https://www.psychologytoday.com/us/blog/hard-realities/201301/how-do-children-comprehend-the-concept-death

Grossman, J., Clark, D., Gross, D., Halstead, L., Pennington, J. (1995). Child bereavement after paternal suicide. *J Child Adolesc Psychiatric Nursing*, 8(2): 5-17.

Hardie-Williams, K. (2016). How to help children grieve the death of a parent. *Good Therapy*. https://www.goodtherapy.org/blog/how-to-help-children-grieve-death-of-parent-1212165

Hatter, B. (1996). Children and the death of a parent or grandparent. In Corr, C. and Corr, D. (Ed.), Handbook of childhood death and bereavement, pp. 131-140. New York: Springer.

Heikes, K. (1997). Parental suicide: A systems perspective. *Bulletin of the Menninger Clinic*, 61(3) 354-367.

Holohan, M. (2018). Experts explain how to talk about suicide with kids by age. https://www.today.com/parents/experts-explain-how-talk-about-suicide-kids-age-t130589

Hurley, D. (1991). The crisis of parental suicide. In N. B. Webb (Ed.)., Play therapy with children in crisis: A casebook for practitioners, pp. 237-253. New York: Scribner's.

Kashani, J., Suarez, L., Luchene, L., & Reid, J. (1998). Family characteristics and behavior problems of suicidal and non-suicidal children and adolescents. *Child Psychiatry and Human Development*, 29(2): 157-168.

Kennebeck, S and Bonin, L. (2019). Suicidal behavior in children and adolescents: Epidemiology and risk factors. https://www.uptodate.com/contents/suicidal-behavior-in-children-and-adolescents-epidemiology-and-risk-factors Accessed: January 15, 2020.

Kids Health. (2017). Bereavement Reactions of Children & Young People By Age Group. https://www.kidshealth.org.nz/bereavement-reactions-children-young-people-age-group

Koplewicz, H. (2017). When a parent commits suicide: A psychiatrist's advice. https://www.thedailybeast.com/when-a-parent-commits-suicide-a-psychiatrists-advice

Lerner, R. (2018). Concepts and theories of human development (4th Ed.). Routledge Taylor and Francis Group.

Marttunen, M., Aro, H., & Lonnqvist, J. (1993). Precipitant stressors in adolescent suicide. *J Am Acad Child Adolesc Psychiatry*, 32(6): 1178-83.

McIntosh, J. (1997). Suicide Survivors. Presented at the American Association of Suicidology Conference, Memphis, TN, April 23-26.

Mishara, B. (2010). Conceptions of death and suicide in children ages 6-12 and their implications for suicide prevention. https://www.onlinelibrary.wiley.com/doi/abs/10.1111/j.1943-278X.1999.tb01049.x

National Institute of Mental Health. (2017). Suicide prevention. Washington, D.C. https://www.nimh.nih.gov/health/topics/suicide-prevention/index.shtml

O'Toole, D. 1994. Growing through grief: A K-12 curriculum to help young people through all kinds of loss. Burnsville, NC: Compassion Books

Parkin, R. & Dunne-Maxim, K. (1995). Child survivors of suicide: A guidebook for those who care for them. New Jersey.

Pfeffer, C., Martins, P., Mann, J., Sunkenberg, M., Ice, A., Damore, J., Gallo, C., Karpenos, I., and Jiang, H. (1997). Child survivors of suicide: Psychosocial characteristics. *Journal of the American Academy of Child and Adolescent Psychiatry*, 36(1), 65-74.

Potter, L. (1998). Suicide in youth: A public health framework – discussion. *Journal of the American Academy of Child and Adolescent Psychiatry*, 37(5), 484.

Ramsay, R., Tanney, B., Tierney, R., Lang. Wm. Suicide Intervention Handbook (2004 10th Ed.). Published by Livingworks.

Range, L. (1996). Suicide and life-threatening behavior in childhood. In Corr, C. and Corr, D. (Ed) Handbook of Childhood Death and Bereavement, pps. 71-88. New York: Springer Publishing.

Ratnarajah, D. and Scofield, M. (2007). Parental suicide and its aftermath: A review. Journal of Family Studies. 13(1): 78-93

Reichel, C. (2019) Suicide prevention: research on successful interventions. https://journalistsresource.org/home/suicide-prevention-research-on-successful-interventions/

Rosenthal, P. and Rosenthal, S. (1984). Suicidal behavior by preschool children. *Am J Psychiatry*, 141(4):520-525.

Salvatore, T. (2018). Suicidal behavior in early childhood and preadolescence. DOI: 10.13140/RG.2.2.23089.43368

Sandler, E. (2016). Talking with kids about suicide. https://www.psychologytoday.com/us/blog/promoting-hope-preventing-suicide/201608/talking-kids-about-suicide

Seguin, M., Lesage, A., & Kiely, M. (1995). Parental bereavement after suicide and accident: A comparative study. *Suicide Life Threat Behavior*, 25(4): 489-92.

Shepard, D., Barraclough, B. (1976). The aftermath of parental suicide for children. *British Journal of Psychiatry*, 129:267-276.

Sinclair, D. and Dangerfield, P. (1998). Human growth after birth. New York: Oxford University Press.

Smith, R. (1993). Life Lessons: Why it's important to talk to your child about death. Sesame Street Parent's Guide, March, 49-51.

Sood, B., Weller, E., Weller, R. & Fristad, M. (1992). Somatic complaints in grieving children. *Comprehensive Mental Health*, 2:17-25.

Speece, M. and Brent, S. (1990). The development of children's understanding of death. In Corr, C. & Corr, D. (Ed)., Handbook of childhood death and bereavement, pp. 29-50. New York: Springer.

Speece, M. and Brent, S. (1992). The acquisition of a mature understanding of three components of the concept of death. Death Studies, 16:211-229.

Stewart, J.G., Shields, G.S., Esposito, E.C. *et al.* (2019). Life Stress and Suicide in Adolescents. *J Abnorm Child Psychol* 47, 1707–1722

Suicide Awareness/Voices of Education (SA\VE). (1996). Explaining suicide to children. SA\VE, Minneapolis, MN.

Suicide Prevention Advocacy Network (SPAN). (1996). Fact sheet: Outcomes of the national awareness day for suicide, May 10.

Tait, D. and Depta, J. (1993). Play therapy group for bereaved children. In N. B. Webb (Ed)., Helping bereaved children: A handbook for practitioners, pp. 169-185. New York: Guilford.

Townley, K. and Thornburg, K. (1980). Maturation of the concept of death in elementary school children. *Educational Research Quarterly*, 5:17-24.

Tracy, N. (2015). Why do teens commit suicide? Cases of teen suicide. Healthy Place. Retrieved on 2019, November: http:// healthyplace.com/ suicide/why-do-teens-commit-suicide-causes-of-teen-suicide

Webb, N. (1993a). Suicidal death of mother: Cases of silence and stigma. In N. B. Webb (Ed). Helping bereaved children: A handbook for practitioners, pp. 137-155. New York: Guilford.

Webb, N. (1993b). Assessment of the bereaved child. In N. B. Webb (Ed). Helping bereaved children: A handbook for practitioners, pp. 19-42. New York: Guilford.

Weller, E., Weller, R., Fristad, M., Cain, S., & Bowes, J. (1988). Should children attend their parent's funeral? *Journal of the American Academy of Child and Adolescent Psychiatry*, 27:559-562.

I wait for the emptiness to drain the weight of loss from my veins

So the sun can move from behind the clouds

And spread new rays of joy

Author Biographies

Carol Hart Hoyt began her career as a psychiatric nurse for the Veterans Hospital in North Little Rock Arkansas having obtained her Registered Nurse credential from St. Vincent Hospital Nursing Program in 1964. She married high school sweetheart, Edd Hoyt in 1964. As their family grew, she retired from nursing to focus on raising three boys, Edd Jr., Keith, and Todd. She later became the owner of a local antique shop, *Suite Inspirations*; furthering her interests in interior design, as well as her marketing and management skills. She sold the shop to focus on raising their son's child, Garrett after the death by suicide of his father, Edd Jr. in 1994.This book chronicles their experiences and lessons learned raising Garrett from an eighteen-month-old baby to a successful young man with a family of his own. She and Edd live in Cabot, Arkansas near sons Keith and Garrett and several of the grand-children and great-grandchildren.

Susan Hart-Hester completed undergraduate and master's degrees in psychology. She completed a doctoral degree in Special Education at the University of Virginia prior to working in the healthcare industry. She began her career working in early childhood development, teaching pre-school age children with autism and other special challenges. She served as a grant writer for over twenty years before moving into workforce development and educational programming. Currently retired, Susan lives in Mississippi where she enjoys writing and serving her community.